STILL ᠆...

Oksana Maksymchuk was born in Lviv, Ukraine, in 1982. She is the author of two award-winning poetry collections, *Xenia* and *Lovy*, in the Ukrainian, as well as a co-editor of *Words for War: New Poems from Ukraine*, an anthology of contemporary poetry. Her English-language poems have appeared in *The Irish Times*, *The London Magazine*, *The Paris Review*, *Poetry London*, *PN Review*, *The Poetry Review* and elsewhere. Oksana was a recipient of a National Endowment for the Arts translation fellowship and a winner of the Scaglione Prize from the Modern Language Association of America, the Peterson Translated Book Award, the American Association for Ukrainian Studies Translation Prize, the Richmond Lattimore Prize, and the Joseph Brodsky/Stephen Spender Prize. She holds a PhD in ancient philosophy from Northwestern University. In recent years, Oksana has been dividing her time between her home in Lviv, the United States, and Europe.

Still
City

DIARY OF AN INVASION

OKSANA MAKSYMCHUK

FOREWORD BY SASHA DUGDALE

CARCANET POETRY

First published in Great Britain in 2024 by
Carcanet
Alliance House, 30 Cross Street
Manchester, M2 7AQ
www.carcanet.co.uk

ISBN 978 1 80017 402 3

Book design by Andrew Latimer, Carcanet
Typesetting by LiteBook Prepress Services
Printed in Great Britain by SRP Ltd, Exeter, Devon

The publisher acknowledges financial
assistance from Arts Council England.

CONTENTS

On 24 February 2022 Russia launched a full-scale invasion of Ukraine. For months beforehand Ukrainians had been expecting and preparing for total war — and yet, when the invasion came, it was still deeply shocking. Ukraine, a modern European country with its cafes and multiplexes, delivery apps and out-of-town industrial estates, was tipped overnight into a war of medieval brutality. As the hours passed and the columns of Russian tanks advanced, it became clear that the hideous deeds of that one single day would take many lifetimes to set right. Now, of course, with the painful benefit of hindsight, it is clear that on 24 February 2022 history turned a corner, and a long period of peace and stability ended in Europe. Ukraine has borne and continues to bear the brunt of this shift towards bloody conflict and tyranny, its daily casualties are victims of Russia's murderous drive to destroy what will never belong to it.

Still City: Diary of an Invasion captures the thoughts and images of the months just before and after the Russian invasion. Oksana Maksymchuk and her family were in her hometown of Lviv in February 2024, and in a recent interview with the poet Rachel Galvin, she spoke of the sense of general disbelief in the months leading up to war: 'But what our own grandparents experienced in the late thirties and forties — the destruction of cities and towns, the execution and torture of civilians, the millions of refugees — it was inconceivable that it could happen within our lifetimes.' The struggle to grasp the 'inconceivable' in order to protect oneself and one's family is one of many cognitive dissonances driving Maksymchuk's lyric: 'Don't / wait for the moment / presently thought impossible...' she writes of siege and flight.

Maksymchuk's tense lyric pieces, their judicious line breaks, their silences, lend themselves admirably to the psychological contradictions of conflict: the earlier poems in *Still City* reflect on the incredulous modern European sensibility, faced with something as ancient and unyielding as military brutality, and on the surprising adaptability of this modern sensibility as it sloughs off its peacetime habits and begins to count the costs of survival. Maksymchuk, a teacher of philosophy as well as a poet, is accustomed to scrutinising the making of thought and has an enviable gift for communicating in images the psychological state of a person being slowly drawn into the state of war: the fleeting impulses, the private arguments with oneself, the stages of acceptance, and the knowledge that this acceptance of the possibility of death and destruction in itself feels like a corruption of the soul, a de-civilising.

As soon as we imagine our cities under fire and their human networks attenuated and destroyed, something has changed in our souls, a change that touches poetic language like an electric shock so that even the word 'soul' swerves 'like an atom' travelling through a void. The real and present becomes vague and contingent, only the plausibility of the bullet, the rocket, the ending, is a certainty.

There is something of Anna Swir's short war poems in the detachment of the speaker in *Still City*. Like Swir, Maksymchuk states the facts of a situation with sharp defiance, an abhorrence of euphemism, unwillingness, or inability to turn away from the irreconcilable: death and life, wonder and grief, are drawn into unholy association. And, like Swir, or the English war poet Keith Douglas, Maksymchuk is a master at shaping the lyric encounter with death, so that artfulnesss and poignancy are maximised. Wryness, even a sort of grim humour, play a part in the encounter: after all, the more one considers the stark ironies of human existence, the more one resembles Lear's Fool. Walter Benjamin once wrote that the 'pure joke' is the essential inner side of mourning — from time to time, like the lining of a dress at its hem or lapel, it makes its presence felt. The 'pure joke' of the masterly poem 'Rocket in the Room', is expressed in the nursery-rhyme alliteration of the title: rockets and children have nothing in common, except, in this murderous case, their location.

Writerly artfulness, its role in shaping experience, itself comes under the poet's careful scrutiny. Maksymchuk is a poet first and foremost, rather than a witness. The poems are made for poetic effect, adjusted, pared back, the *mot juste* selected. How does this essentially sensual and cerebral labour sit with the moral imperatives of war and suffering nationhood? How can the poet bring forth a poem (creaturely, immoral):

> Like a stag, erect, farouche
> a poem stands, listens for the explosions
> so far-off they seem but a memory
> a hallucination

There are no answers to this question, except perhaps in the assertion of life, the dance in the face of war and death. A dance which she describes as

> ... the kind that irradiates
> every surviving nucleus
> rendering you a creature
>
> absolutely new
> facing the passage of time
> naked and unashamed

*

Russian territorial aggression against Ukraine began with the annexation of Crimea in 2014, and conflict broke out in the Donbas in that same year, so Maksymchuk has had the vivid experience of her compatriots in the East, their poetic expression of war, flight and occupation to shape her poetic imagination. She describes their writing as part of her own literary DNA: she translated and edited (together with Max Rosochinsky) the authoritative anthology of war poetry from this period *Words for War* (Academic Studies Press, 2017), as well as full collections by Lyuba Yakimchuk and Marianna Kiyanovska. In an interview for *PN Review* 272, I asked her about her choice to write about the war in English, given her translations and her own acclaimed poetry written and published in Ukrainian. She replied that writing in English created 'the illusion of temporal distance, which allows me to speak in a freer, more even voice', explaining that her Ukrainian poetry is more formally constrained, syllabo-tonic, tightly rhymed and with the overt technical mastery that is a feature of even contemporary Ukrainian poetics. Her adopted language, English, and perhaps more specifically US English, allowed more playfulness and a gap of creative potential into which she could insert an immigrant identity and voice.

These poems, then, are not translations from Ukrainian, but parallel tracks. They do not exist in Ukrainian, although even in their free verse shaping there is a formidable sense of poise and control and a bright clarity of narrative: a belief in the lyric's ability to convey trauma. This, at least to me, denotes the shadowy presence of another poetic tradition. Maksymchuk notes in the same interview that when she left Ukraine for the States in her teens, absence closed in around the world she had lost, and by writing poetry she could create traces: tracks she could follow back.

I'm struck by the renewal of the lyric form to express the psychology and philosophy of a world in extremis. I've read a great deal of Ukrainian poetry (much of it in Oksana's translations) and its greatest gift to us, its readers and poets outside Ukraine, is the faith it places in poetry to record, like a barometer, the 'swerving' of the soul. In this matter Oksana Maksymchuk is doubtless part of the Ukrainian poetic renaissance. She is unusual in harnessing English for the purpose, but we should be glad and grateful she does — it may still seem inconceivable to us, but our world, too, is changed by

> ... an explosion rushing
> into the distant regions
> where there's no desire, no strife, no war

Sasha Dugdale

STILL CITY

INTIMATE RELATIONSHIP

I bought a hat
of faux mink fur
to wear in the war

In my hat I sit
in my cellar
waiting

The enemy's late
I read his messages
on my phone

popping open
jars of strawberry jam
lining the cellar walls

Like a lover
my enemy sends me
flowers, emojis, words

of condolence
supplications, doctored
screenshots, explicit photos

THE FOURTH WALL

No collapse, just a gradual shrinking
of the present

like a novel adapted into a play
within the four walls

showing outlines of meadows, bridges
fluttering shadows

Life goes on

the future
menacingly open

An air-raid siren
begins to wail

How many today?

We stop what we're doing
stand by the curtain, our eyes

on the sky, fearing

how normal it all now feels
how boring

WARM, WARMER

Awaiting its arrival
I bide my time
knitting a single sock

The cat plays
with the ball of yarn
rolls it like a grenade

Friends stop by
drunk on wine
bearing gifts:

greasy slabs with blue
veining — secret roadmaps
traced off a living body

winter fruit
our families couldn't afford
when we were kids

Huddled up under blankets
we watch new movies
from abroad

silence punctuated by phones
humming & lighting up
with a refrain

Are they here yet?

EMERGENCY BAG

Pack all you need to survive
in the wild, in the snow, in the cellar
two three four five days

Don't
wait for the moment
presently thought impossible:

When a city
resounds with sirens or falls —
suddenly — silent

When a street
catches fire, fills with
smoke

When the windows break
the walls collapse
the lights go off

When the men at the door
shout: *Quick Quick*
The transport's waiting

STOLEN TIME

Trapped in a plan
of another's making
we're squandering time
awaiting the war

Perfectly formed evenings
of navigating between the dark
silhouettes of trees
against the purple snow

Weekend afternoons of
urgent love-making, voices
seeping through half-drawn curtains
adorned by shadows of

migratory birds —
jubilant and remote
citizens of a world
shared in shards

COLLECTIVE BARGAINING

On New Year's Eve we record wishes
on strips of paper, burn them, then
gulp down the ashes
chasing them with cheap
sweet champagne

Will those who survive
be us
or our shadows
beings transformed
altered?

If I come out of the ordeal
unharmed
I will burn each day
in a celebration
I'll be fearless and defiant

I promise
the higher power
trying, again, to take
a private exit
out of the common catastrophe —

typical of our species

AMOR FATI

Googling the daily news
for the number of troops
gathered at the border

Dillydallying
reorganising books
battling the dust bunnies

Waltzing around the hallway
with a disgruntled cat
to the music of running water

A finite set of parts
like shards of glass
inside a kaleidoscope —

a fragile symmetry
irradiated by blasts, explosions
reaching in blinding waves

out of the future

REVERSALS

A shirt turned inside out retains the shape
of a torso, matching it in form

A home turned inside out — not a skeleton, but a pile of rubble
brought by gravity to a resting point

A body turned inside out is a spectacle
resembling a bag spilling its private content

A mountain turned inside out
is still a mountain

WHEN A MISSILE FINDS A HOME

Cat in the window
examines the snowflakes that float —
marks of art in the winter dark

It's a Christmas Eve in my homeland
the things to come
waiting to be unwrapped

in a house with a roof
not yet stuffed with snow, openings
still windows and doors

I remember the poet who wrote
of a missile
entering his home

For him in Donbas
all the newness is over
and yet

Vasya the cat in his lap
licks his face
just like it used to

Mom gets ready for work in the kissel-blue
glow of dawn while he reads
verses of Mandelstam

in a room
they patched up with
foam, scotch tape & cardboard

How he dreamt of becoming the Minister of
Culture in the new state, orchestrating
massive screenings of Eisenstein!

His defenders said: No use for culture now!
Better take this gun!
Fatten up the Motherland on some blood!

It's all over for him —
the wait, the uncertainty —
What will become of me?

Just the beginning for us

SEVERAL CIRCLES

What I see is an eye
while you're seeing
a female breast
purple nipple on top
like a cherry

Stubbornly phenomenal
circles join, overlap
sending each mind
on its own
lonely journey

So Kandinsky and Klee
sat in each other's lap
for a little while
in a house they shared
in Dessau

as outside the frame
yet another shape
shed its flesh
exposing the blackened spine
of a rising, inverted star

Here, beloved —
taste my eyeball
rinsed in a special cocktail
only I can craft
in my mortal body

WAR-SHY

In a country bled
for a decade, we sip wine
in a room with a warm dessert
homemade pie, custard
with a real vanilla bean

Friends of friends have died
on the frontline
locked up in cellars
buried alive
in their own beds

We mourn them online
startled, surprised
as if shaken out of sleep
by an explosion
around the corner

So alien — this war
secreted and remote
a presence you sense
with your gut and spine
not daring to witness

UNGENTLE REMINDER

when my fluttering heart
takes off
its awkward perch
within my ribcage

let me at least remind you
to button up your coat
and put on the red hat
I got online

to help identify you
in the current of the crowd
in case the enemy strikes
by air, by land, by water

ARGUMENTS FOR PEACE

How could there be a war in this city with
cobblestone streets, glowing stars
in the windows, festive
dogs in felt deer antlers?

In a central park, children sled
down the hills, making sharp joyful noises
and the clusters of snow that fall
cover up their tracks, landing gently
on hands and faces

Perfectly formed cakes
in the lit display cases
are yet more proof
of the goodness of the universe

In the glowing interiors, we dip
noses in whipping cream
on purpose, and pretend not to notice
when somebody's phone lights up with
a face of a foreign leader
warning of invasion

What's a missile to do with
a concert hall full of children?

What's an air raid to do with
a holiday celebration?

With glasses of sparkling wine
we gather around lit trees

We say it couldn't be

War wouldn't dare come
seeing how happy we are
how good our lives
and all that we've got to lose

We love our children too much
We love our homes too much

and so, we argue, time and again

there'll be no war
there'll be no war

RECONFIGURED CONNECTIONS

My cousin writes
she's in a cellar
with her one-year-old
her husband mobilised

The baby, she used to be scared
of explosions —
now they lull her
to sleep

She sends a video she made
when she sneaked out
to draw some water
from a well

In the distance — an opening up
instant freedom from
order and gravity
then a fall, a settling

Our town, it may look like a heap
of rubble now
but it's made of the same stuff —
only the form has changed

I read her messages on my phone
then piss into a bottle
set it in the corner of
my own bomb shelter

DUCK AND COVER

Separated from my child
on the inner lip of what's yet to come
I can't find a point for my soul to balance
I imagine terrible things happening

Terrible things are happening, mom

He sends a pic of his classroom, desks
abandoned in haste, neon gadgets
spilling, books spread out
on the floor like fallen birds

Will I see you again? sounds
in the back of my mind —
and I pinch myself

Through catastrophes
I still seek your hand
even if there is no safety

as we await the bombs
windows crisscrossed with tape, floors
covered with walnuts that dry
all year, back doors

barricaded with boxes of
chocolates, sacks of
sugar, potatoes, small
wrinkled apples

WHAT GIVES

From a war — can you hide
in a wardrobe?

From a tank — take cover
behind a bookcase?

Will a song keep you safe
when the ceiling caves?

Could a metaphor sniff you out
in the rubble?

And this poem you're inside —
won't it need a lock?

Does it follow the law
of four walls, a monad

with no windows, no
secret openings?

HOUSE ARREST

I've been writing this note
for a couple of minutes now
Still there's no response
I'm so angry

A vision came
bearing a gift
It was moist and sweet
smelling faintly of plumbum

How dare you abandon me
alone in a room
in a house with strangers
in a city popping with guns

All that keeps me whole
is the memory of the meal we share
every Friday night
and the candles we light

Promise we'll make it again
peeling roots
in the kitchen, stained hands
passing a knife, a potato

The room forms
around me, listening in
to my fear
and not as a friend

Under its oculus, I strip
naked, I whirl, my heavy wings
rustling with each *plié*
like lowered shutters

CHERRY ORCHARD

A poet on the other side
of the war
writes: brothers and sisters fly up
into immortality

Was it years or days ago
that we read our poems
in an underground gallery
surrounded by feminist art
to an audience of teenagers?

Drunk on wine
by the fountain in City Square
we laughed so hard
that a window opened
and a woman in a nightgown
shook both her fists at us!

Time to go, poetesses
you said, and we shared a kiss
that could land us in prison
in Mordovia

Now we each have a cellar
in which to hide
from bombs & aerial strikes

I wonder what supplies
you stocked up on

Are they the same as mine?

On your Facebook profile
a slogan: 'Motherland is
everything, everything else is —
Nothing'

I scroll through your timeline, popping open
the jar of jam I'd been saving for
a rainy day

a gift from your hometown
no longer a place but
a name
on a map, a ridge of rubble

CONTACT

From within a solitude
of a fate you can choose but
cannot share —

we exchange words
cross swords
made of recycled plastic

Here and there — an echo
of a forgotten ritual
that once meant something:

a handshake, a kiss
palms folded together
in supplication

If I respond in kind, it's because
I'm an imposter, adjusting to
local custom

Inside, who am I?
A steady bubbling
raised to a pitch so high

that cats leave the room
and no dog dares look me
in the eye

PARTING

Who said you'd have a parting of
substances smooth as
parting of lips to draw a breath
for a final song?

Who painted for you: a swan
a swallow, the thorn birds
hungry for death's
penetrating horn?

Free of fear, you'll be received
clean like a slate, levitating
into Tarkovsky's *Mirror* —
whoever promised?

As the news of shootings and
missile strikes shatters
the hiding places
of our minds

words for 'soul' and 'save'
swerve like atoms
traveling through the void
maddeningly colliding

THE ORDERS OF PRIORITY

World is a poem
before it's anything else
unfolding out of an opening —

not yet a word but a low
steady buzzing, aglow
with a future plenitude

Love is as old as strife
Final causes are also first
Being is before time —
so ontology precedes
temporality

And the poem I'm crafting
at this very instant
before your eyes

(bracket off the sound
of my laboured breathing
as the air raid siren lows)

yes
it is, for a moment, last
in the sequence of things

that come to be
reach their peak, perish
defy forgetting

THE CAT'S ODYSSEY

Our emergency suitcase packed
we consider the cat
watching us from across the room

Do we leave her behind?
Do we schlep her across the border?

Online, I view ads of backpacks
with a clear protruding bubble

window — the face of the cat inside
small and surprised

like the face of an astronaut
carried into

the outer space

COMMERCIAL BREAK

Meet the Tourniquet —
your companion for any adventure

Outdoor missions, expeditions
to resupply and restock

Get all you need
in a single trip

Make him a permanent
inhabitant of Emergency Bag

A reliable saviour!
A metaphysical miracle!

His inhuman grip
will keep your blood in

even as you're uncorked
like a bottle of wine

flipped upside down

PEGMAN

If I die
in the war
bury me on Maps

I'm looking for a quiet spot
in a village with a name that smells of mushrooms
under the fallen leaves
whorling roots, fruits that stay on trees
in the wintertime, wild fermented berries
locals turn into wine

Drop the pegman there
in the zone
vacant yet sharable, amid
phantoms of trunks with missing limbs
startled half-empty streets
blurry faces of passers-by

Visit me every night
if you wish, before logging off
your grainy figure
holding a tight bouquet
of forget-me-nots, casting no shadow
on sullen boughs

I reserve the right
to respawn

POST-TRUTH

Some say it didn't happen
Others that it was staged

Corpses from morgues, laid out
for an exhibition

Look how artful their arrangement
as if curated by someone

with an eye for effects
opaquely gruesome, darkly erotic

You see what you see

but there's reason for doubt
always—room for deception

It looks bad but isn't
Sounds bad, but they're lying

In any case, how do you know
you didn't dream it all up
some terrible night
drinking and vomiting

until blackout?

STILL LIFE OF A PERSON WITH A PUG

She was walking her pug
down the street in a town
where she spent her childhood
and teenage years

still in her winter coat
even though it was getting
warmer, and the buds on the poplars
grew engorged

Something bit her
in the back, and she fell
and lay there
on the sidewalk

The next day, a neighbour brought out
a sheet with tiny roses
for that which was once her body
a matching pillowcase for the pug's

A passer-by took a photograph
and posted it on Telegram
causing an avalanche of
angry emojis

WATER UNDER THE BRIDGE

No more bridge now
but the river
flows as it did before

like a single tear
rolls down the face
of the landscape

tears through the terrain
laid out for it by another tear
and another before it

Doesn't grieve when the towns
clustered along its banks
lie in ruins

Doesn't weep
cradling the corpses
toying with the remains

Indiscriminate
like a poem's flow

reflecting everything
changing nothing

DRONE FOOTAGE

When a shell strikes a person
there's a scattering

resembling a flock of birds
taking off

hands flying in the air
signalling

feet levitating
in mid-kick

their avian shapes
casting shadows

lithe and carefree
from on high

ROCKET IN THE ROOM

what the rocket has in common
with the room full of children
is its current location

somebody thought the rocket
belonged in the room with children
and now it's here

in time
someone else will come
and collect the pieces

of the rocket and of the children
weeping and shouting insults
at the sky

but for now
this rocket and these children
are an unsorted matter

a puzzle
awaiting a solution

MUTED BELL

For whom — the death tolls
arrangements of pixels expressing
not tragedy but —
veritable information?

For whom — neon clusters of
heat, a secret mycelium
under a shattered museum
turned to a mausoleum?

For whom — curled-up bodies
set out in the street to cool
dusted like donuts
with falling snow?

Drawn to the blooms of
slow-opening wounds
thirsting for nectar
like eager bees

these words —
for whom?

MEMENTO

I try on forgetting like
a new pair of shoes

In the mirror, lights
slightly flickering —
it appears
almost tolerable

Yet when the lights go out
it pinches and gnaws
stabs and corrodes —
a sizzling acid

Rage rises from soles
to my throat
like a foaming stream

I let out
scream after scream

My feet are bleeding
and so are my teeth

ROSE

It can't happen to me
until it does

The trajectories meet
on point

Terror comes off
layer by layer

Glowing inside
the cellar

supple serrated petals
pushing against the war

here it is — the Rose
I'm dancing here

A LULLABY WITH NO THEODICY

You're beautiful

as a hand that waves hello
in a window crisscrossed
with tape, still intact
from a blast wave

as a whiff of perfume
in the belly of the metro where
sleepy civilians shelter in place
during the rocket strikes

as a loaf of bread, solid and firm
handed by a masked person
in a uniform without insignia
out of an armoured vehicle

as a charged phone
that still has reception — inside it
a loved one's voice
echoing in a distant refuge

as an hour of electricity and running
water in a city littered with
dusty backpacks and tents of
a clamouring foreign army

TEMPO

What I didn't suspect about
war is that there'd be
music

Not the kind that compels you to move
in harmonious discord
with the others

Nor the kind that creates a burning
in the loins to mix breath
with breath

But the kind that irradiates
every surviving nucleus
rendering you a creature

absolutely new
facing the passage of time
naked and unashamed

In the intervals between
war and worse, we discern the score
ready to whirl with

planets and stars that coil
around our fragile core
orderly and composed

like a tragic chorus

A GUEST FROM AFAR

In a bed we set up
on the floor
in the hallway, where the walls
are most solid
with no windows to burst
she rolls into a ball
and falls & falls
not hearing her own sobs
she's grown so used to them

Packing and hauling bags
throwing bags over tracks
suitcases and small bundles
of severed arms, hands
straining to sign
some desperate last message:
the name of a loved one
instructions for making
Grandma's heirloom pie

In the serpentine cellar
that's now her mind, she expands
testing the possible exits
with the outer limits
of her own body, exposed
bare flesh

SUPPLICATION IN THE RUINS

Moist and supple, this path
underfoot

soiled crusty patches — isles
of friction in an unbroken line

The sky rests on the eye
cleared out and hallowed

like a room sitting empty
in a city deoccupied

Overflowing with anxious longing
Let us live, I whisper

into a cleft in a rock, a hollow
of a tree, a hole

of a groundhog's den

TIMELINE SCROLL

A pretty Midwesterner on vacation, exploring
Venice for the first time

A handsome poet, her photographs
shot by another less famous poet

An ad for learning a foreign language

A friend whose house got destroyed
by a foreign missile last night

An ad for pizza delivery

A friend whose account's in a coma —
she fell in a coma

last week while trying to order pizza
last words on her mind, probably

'cheese, pepperoni, olives'

Not 'war', not 'rocket'

An ad for 'rocket'

TREES

In the years of occupation
he painted trees

Dead trees, fallen trees
trees with lesions

marking the place in the bark
where dying happens

Tree silhouettes in a line
facing a firing squad of trees

Trees standing up to their necks
in still flood water

Solemn trees, raving trees
trees with their tongues torn out

Shimmering trees, dreamy trees
trees voluptuous and upright

stubbornly transforming
even the dimmest light

into something sweet
trapping it

in the sprawling roots —
hidden inverted networks

rippling underground, radiating out

MARQUISE OF O

When they dragged her out
of the cellar
she lost consciousness

only coming to
flashes of light
the sounds of voices

that bounced against her
like hard tennis balls
unstoppable

By the hoarseness in her throat
she recognised she was screaming
as if through a deep sleep

Two months later, when the verdict
was read by a foreign doctor
she cried in surprise

How could it be?

Nothing happened to her
but a dream!

And wouldn't anyone
suffer from night terrors

lulled to sleep by the sirens
on the floor of a cellar
listening for explosions?

BEYOND THE VISIBLE

On the other side
of the door that opens
only in one direction

as the city below folds into
a smaller and smaller space
watch the sky expand outward, growing

ever larger — an explosion rushing
into the distant regions
where there's no desire, no strife, no war

Still long visible
after the town is no more —

a mushrooming cloud
of splattered glitter

LINING UP THE CROSSHAIRS

> *How slow life is*
> *How violent hope is*
> *— Guillaume Apollinaire*

What the poet saw in the future is
a meekness, a pliability — yet it spat him out
not with a burst of shrapnel but
as a plague setting off

fireworks in his lungs:
Look how bright, my love
and it bruises —
like a kiss!

Tearing forms from the inside
time refuses, again
to remain contained, demands
an expression suitable to its violence

Like a stag, erect, farouche
a poem stands, listens for the explosions
so far-off they seem but a memory
a hallucination

From the distance of art, we strive
to define the features
of our time, and the future defies our edit
stubbornly, definitively

ALGORITHMIC MELTDOWN

I don't know if the images of
bombings are what you yearn for
in your feed

Scrolling on my phone, I too prefer
funny puppy videos
flowers and minerals, food porn

Instead, I see pictures of ruins
blackened privates exposed
puddles of glass

Somebody's liver
smeared over the asphalt
like melted ghee

Somebody's daughter
sandwiched between the slabs
of concrete

Sight, the philosopher said, is first
of the senses, it reigns supreme
making sense of things

As I hover over the images —
toggling between the close-ups
and 'dollhouse view'

peering into cracked mirrors
wedging doors with my cursor
what do I hope

to unsee?

ORPHIC EUPHEMISMS

We say she died
but really, she got killed

slaughtered along with others
at the unlikely location

of sacrifice

A small black cloud
swallowed her whole

spat out only a husk of body

that couldn't wake up
no matter how hard it tried

... The eye of the bluest pigment
seeks the sky

to dip into, and finds:
cool folds of flesh

shut like a metal door

But what of celestial seed?

It too finds a fold, a furrow
to hide in —

until next time

THE PRODIGALITY OF SUFFERING

In the dictionary of victims
there's no space
for a hair to fall

Chance
wresting crumbs of freedom
from necessity

Future frothing with mirth
mingling
milk and blood

Always — an altar
and always —
a lamb

Always someone
leading the lamb
to the altar

Always — hands
clasped together
that say: I'm bound

Always — fingers
testing the point
the blade

as if pausing
to question
the mechanisms of exchange:

that all suffering's
for the greater good

that all wrongs are redeemed
in the afterlife

that through love
the world is restored, renewed

when it plunges into a cleansing
frenzy of violence

THE REMAINS OF A UNIVERSE

What is most important
to some living being
is now in the back
of a truck

speeding through seething steppe
in a bag
with a U-shaped zipper
and a handle

inside it another bag
much smaller
holding a hand
and some loose digits

WILL TO GROW

Where bullets now fall
blooms will rise

In the early spring — snowdrops
lily of the valley, willow branches with fuzzy buds
resembling baby bunnies

Later — tulip, narcissus, crocus
boughs of lilac adorning
fences and ruined gardens

In the summer — poppies, bruising easily
prickly ears of wheat
Vermeer-blue cornflowers

In the fall — marigolds, neon-bright chrysanthemums
sunflowers, ripened discs heavy with
titmice and sparrows

In the winter — blood-speckled bunches of guelder rose
snowberry strands beaded with
taut white fruit that pops underfoot

like tiny mines

DEGREES OF SEPARATION

By the time it is over some of us will
die, many of us will watch
loved ones die

most of us will watch
loved ones watch
their loved ones die

connecting us all
pearl by pallid pearl
gem by bleeding gem

From a distance of words
in the frame of a blank-faced page
you too bear witness to

the interminable

THE HEAD OF ORPHEUS

> *Power, repulsive as*
> *hands of a barber*
> *— Osip Mandelstam*

Butchers and tyrants —
they too know poetry

grabbing hold of
the throats that paddle

truth in and out
of lungs, like contraband

fleshy folds come together
in sweet vibrations

Prone to lose their minds
maddened by orphic breathing

bacchants, somnambules
in the no-place of power

tear open the secret quarters where
words are welded from elements

As for the voices thrown
in the service of violence —

they also cannot escape
their unmusical master

monstrous severed heads
buried in the sand

mouthing verses
unintelligible, barbaric

CRITICAL FEELING

Before we proceed
let us complete an exercise
in critical feeling

Feeling is critical
when you suspend a feeling
you don't feel with certainty

You've got to separate
the true from the false
sifting out the husks

When you begin to slide
extend your talons
into the slippery slope

In a sea of red herrings
raise the tiny white flag
out of your floating eye

TRANSFER OF KNOWLEDGE UNDER THE OCCUPATION

As the battles raged on
he transformed
and crawled and crawled
the walls of the room

Eating garbage was second nature
Dutifully, he consumed
what leftovers he found
in the bins in the dark

His unheated room
witnessed scenes of
solitary lust, lucid chitin stretching
with a humourless pleasure

Absolutely not
to be seen or heard
the city of his youth
crawling with hostiles

he peeked out the window
his six nervous hands
grasping the curtain
on which he hung

In the night, he sneaked out
to roam, troubling his hosts
raiding their collection of
sugar cubes

MIRRORING

Blasts from afar
reach in waves
of liquified light

and the muses
are sirens

We've been shaken
before, and now
practiced in bowing down

we puff our cheeks
and blow!

From a distance so great
terror is a flame
over a thin church candle —

it goes out
like a passing thought

Don't pour wax
in your ear, stranger —
it'll seal your soul

Children outside
play war

War plays along
with the children, tossing them
like fruit

forcing rot
into a pip-lined core

UNFINISHED MISSIVES

That I need to imagine you
sound and alive
tells about how I survive
absences, dearest mama

ellipses in perceiving
filled with the humming of
fading connection, a hopeful drumming
of dots and dashes...

How could you ever reply
to this letter I cannot send —
nobody trusted to take it
to your hideout?

You may ask this, squinting
your eyes, as if inquiring
about the stash of smokes
I hid under a floorboard

Mama, this is how
you respond to me
when you're not here —
setting my soul in motion

not as a virtual automaton
of a Cartesian nightmare
but as another mind
resolutely autonomous

Reaching out, I touch —
your hands, compact
crustacean wrists, brightly
enamelled talons

A MUSEUM OF RESCUED OBJECTS

In the months preceding the unspeakable I hoarded
food and supplies from across the country
following the script I'd inherited from my grandmother
and her grandmother before her
so immediately felt — it seemed instinctual

The pale mohair scarf
arrived from Kharkiv — brought out of confinement
in a lacquered wardrobe, pristine, with a tag
indicating its price in Soviet rubles
An unwanted gift or a prized possession?

The kilo of mint from Mariupol
came in a box the size of a small coffin
Full of flowers and weeds, it had been
not picked — but cut down
with a scythe or a sickle

From Kherson I received candied pinecones
bitterer than I remembered, sharply
fragrant, taking me back to the woods
where grandpa and I harvested them in silence
not to tip off the warden

And a set of ornate brown teapots
chugged in from Irpin, the curls of their handles
like the tail of the clay rooster — a symbol of time-keeping
that, months later, survived
in the kitchen blown open — no floor, no ceiling

In my own home
not yet bombed, nor destroyed by a missile
all the objects are whole, breathing in
with relief, secretly
dancing in place

I am not whole
Not home
Hardly dancing, slowly
forgetting
how to breathe

SOUL IS A SIEVE

Day in, day out, I lose
a word or two
from the texts you composed
under the occupation

Here and there, a poem
emerges that mirrors
what you have said —
a ripple of a distortion
changing the dim reflection
with every act of remembering

I forget I forget

Was this the phrase you used
or did I invent it
in this act of translation
between tongue and
language, between
eye and screen, heart
and hand, between your
terror and my inadequacy?

Please forgive me
all I got wrong

every precocious word, each
precious typo

flattened into a poem
like roadkill

IMPROBABLE PORTALS

When a loved one is trapped
in a place too terrible
to enter

I still enter
but close the door
behind me

ADVICE TO A YOUNG POEM

Stay little, poem
fine and sharp like a charm

mysterious
a maker of no sense

Fewer things can go wrong
with fewer lines

Fewer promises break
in fewer words

Little ones trickle out
of the cage through bars

one can barely see, seep
through the capillaries

in a windowless & evasive
mind that's devised

ways to protect itself
against spells and magic

Helpless yet
busily resilient

they form like clouds
woven of gauze and mucus

dealing in recovery of broken
hope, delivery of the forgotten

inessential yet
dear

Little ones, of no weight
are enough

to transform
as one peers into the sky
to the sound of an air raid siren

falls asleep in a bathtub

dances inside
a cellar

SENTENCES

A ten-year-old, escaped
from a city absorbed beyond
a serrated border

writes a name
on a sheet of paper
draws a line

setting apart
the narrative sentences from
the interrogative

I am writing now.
I live abroad.
I have two cats.

When can we go home?
Where is my dad?
What are we to do?

CLUSTERS OF ROSES

Luminous — the ink
pooling in bullet holes
to paint blooms

pain turned to
petals, terror — to
style and stigma

Ovaries fill with
juice, and we too learn:
lives are fragile & can get broken

As for life, it says yes
Always — yes

No use
denying it

REVISIONS

With a sidelong glance, she catches
sight of a red tabby cat
and instantly
as through a wormhole
she's back in the dimly lit hallway
fumbles for keys in her purse
opens the portal to find
an expectant face looking up

Holding the tight
clump of body against her chest
she closes and locks the door
knows there's no point:
the whole place will collapse
in a matter of days
under heavy bombardment

But this one, he's now
with her, he won't
die alone
buried alive under the couch
she just splurged on to celebrate
their amazing new life

Imagine —
a refugee who had managed
to make it out of the zone, built herself up
in a city of strangers, away from
coal mines and land mines, by the seaside
this time. What dreams come to pass!

...She ruffles the fur, lightly touches
the nose, feels the toes
with a trembling hand...

Imagine, my love, imagine

CENTIPEDE

Saw you first as a dark
shadow in the corner
of the borrowed room
where we sleep in a clump
like some animal family
keeping each other warm
the missiles pound
our home back home

Saw you next as a blurry-edged
shape on a wall
taking you for a defect
in its surface
taupe orange peel
resembling a place
where nail punctures plaster —
and gets pushed out

Felt you last
underfoot, as an object supple
and soft, a damp clump of cat
fuzz, an escaped
cotton ball, scurrying under
the dresser where we dumped
what we'd hastily packed —
mismatched socks, underwear & passports

To your yellow spine
peppered with tiny dots, I say
I'm sorry
without thinking whether
you are a person
with ends and reasons and
what my kind owes
to your kind

Hobbling on tiptoe
I do not cry
held together by words
that enclose
two living beings with
sixteen pairs of legs
and four eyes
between us

UNVERIFIED FOOTAGE

Bodies in the street
Scorched trees

Black squares
for windows

Black buttons
for eyes

Hair blown
in the wind, wind

Drones hover
in the wind, wind

Crows take wing
in the wind, wind

War rolls
down the street

like a severed head
a skeletal tumbleweed

spreading its spores
turning everything

to garbage

SURVIVOR SYNDROME

What I couldn't stand to witness
is my fault

What I fled from — my fault —
making use of my absence
to unfold, unfurl

What I closed my eyes to, what
ears couldn't bear, what
I dare not utter & can't recall

Hands that don't stay at home — my fault
Hands that don't know their place
Hands that finger

weapons, hold women down
and unzip pants, hands pressing buttons, pushing
against the boundaries — my fault

What those heartless hands
are up to — isn't it up to me?

I'm raising my face
in an answer to the question —

a coin that fell
to the bottom of the well

MOTHER'S WORK

The remains
buried hastily
in the yard
recently ran about

with a shaggy dog
sewed a dress for a doll
bombed at Scrabble
sang a lullaby

SAMURAI CAT

They will recognise him
by the tattoo of a samurai cat
on his ankle

blackened, yet still
discernible
despite the burns

He sat out for a long time
in the summer heat
before they collected him

When he finally arrives
at his destination
they plead with his mother

not to unzip the bag
showing only
a single foot

Shell-shocked, she obeys
without listening, lips searching
the plastic membrane

NEIGHBOUR

Hurling pebbles over our fence then
running away, his heels
dark from the road dirt
as we waved him back

'Oh come on, come join us!'

The neighbour's kid, always
making trouble for cats, sometimes
reading the works of his countrymen
under the linden tree

Pretty-faced yet
wild as hell, so said
the one girl from our tribe
who had tried to befriend him

Children's games, then
under our grandparents' gaze
Giants, they raised our world
out of dust and rubble!

Now we kids are grown up
our grandparents gone
and the neighbour
he's trying to make a mark

puffy hands
busily stitching up
boys for the mincemeat pie
girls for the red beet soup

into our beds, our hiding places
now and again —
throwing a rock
a rocket

LINGERING LIKENESS

If you make an effigy
of cloth, paper, and sticks
and give it a name
and make it feel loved

I wonder
whether the girl who survived
the same immense blast
in a parallel universe

would feel anything?

BLANK PAGES

> *History is not the soil in which happiness grows.*
> *The periods of happiness in it are the blank pages of history.*
> — *G. W.F. Hegel*

In a story of a life, too, happiness
is a kind of silence
a lacuna of meaning
a sweet ellipsis

No disruptions, dangerous
forks in the road, hard
rocks to hurl, thrills
that shake to the core

In the blessed lull
of unearned, freefalling calm
there are stories to tell
words to form

Weaving verses
out of faint gusts of wind
susurrating branches
filling the pages with

clouds and trees
songbirds calling out of
the thicket, shadows settled
on a beloved face —

things so delicate
and so thin
they barely appear
on the clear film

of a life well-lived
each day a rhyme
for the previous day
synchronised and ordered

PAREIDOLIA

I could be silent now
locked up in a cellar
minding the business of survival
intimate & immediate

And yet, here I am, inside
a song like inside another's
slashed-open gut
keeping warm

in the darkness that falls
billowing out
like an inkblot, an angry
talking cloud

INVOLUNTARY GAMENESS

The nerve of trees lining
the rocky slopes!

Of bombes devoured
in bombed-out cities!

Of flowers, of birds
their contours more vibrant now
against the wreckage

Of children's voices —
a joyful taut cannonade —
rushing in through the windows

shattered by a blast wave

CRIMEA QUINCE

Collected some pine
cones, also made
quince jam

Under a woollen blanket
I paid an arm and a leg for, I hide
my other arm and leg

He writes the place is crawling
with men with guns

He writes we're running
out of water

He writes, we aren't leaving
We'll wait it out in the bomb shelter

Wilting the quince
I neglected to put in sugar
not because I didn't want to

but because I lied
to my future self

It tastes faintly bitter
like that holiday in Crimea
we once shared

before it was occupied

PUPPETS OF GOD

Do I dare
disturb the music
of the universe, its slow-turning
spheres, threads on spindles
meted out by Fates

So the poet raved, impersonating
another poet

How you lied, my beloved!
There's hardly time
for the business of poetry
you insisted was vital

for survival of
what is human inside us

As for what we're doing here
seeding peonies into corpses —
they're devoured by worms
before they sprout

Our zealously mortal souls are
transient episodes
in the life cycle of the humus
mixed with stardust —

a formula so prosaic

my imposter's voice collapses
back into a box —
an embarrassed jack
with a spring for a spine

UNSTEADY TOPOGRAPHY

Even inside a war
I'm still at work
making life delicious

Mutinous pastries rise and fall
like a tidal wave
in the makeshift oven
we've assembled out of loose bricks
in the communal yard —
a collective poem

In a room across the street
now and again, I catch a glimpse of
two elderly neighbours
making love
LED light glowing above them
like the moon

Standing in the full
glare of the war, I'm a surface
reflecting its awesome light
shadows emerging due to
the unusual features
of my own darkened soul

I'm a sucker for sweetness
delicate, frothing streams
creaming the landscape

Yet inside me, mountains crumble
craters open on the papery surface

tall load-bearing cakes
break into a scream

THE WINTER OF OUR DISCO

While I write this letter to you
my beloved
in the winter dusk

with my left hand
then with my right
then with my feet

water in my cup
turns to
a block of ice

I don't mention
pee in the pot
conveniently *en suite*

I write this way
to stay unrecognised
by our time

A HEART HAS A HOME, BUT NOT — A FIST

My cousin's heart stopped on its own
in her own bed, in a worn-out town
occupied by the enemy

At gunpoint for months, her heart fluttered so
she tried to numb it
to keep it from breaking down

A heart that fails to pump blood
is no longer an organ but
a residual matter, a growth

in the shape of a heart
useless, unfunctional —
so a philosopher

But the little girl
pressed to her mother's body
knocked on the chest with a clenched

fist — so that it would awaken, flex
like a red bulbous fish
summoning all its flesh

to its calling:
the singular task
of loving her

PURE POETRY

From an ever-greater distance
I begin to see
what seemed obvious
and thus, not worth mentioning:

What formal paucity
caused me to weed
around words and phrases
I dreamt essential?

What orphic urges pushed me
into creating formulae
for all
that I most desired?

Training my soul
to consume
only the rarest of things
beyond the Divided Line

I barely divined
their materials:
fine mortal tears
raw, wounded matter

Are the sounds uttered
by a head severed
in sacred violence
thereby sweeter?

Are the stanzas clearer
for the absence of
blood, semen, phlegm —
betrayed as traces, as signs?

Now that the muse
is upon me, how do I take
the measure of business
so unmistakably human?

Vanya killed Dima over
the spoils: a Bosch
washing machine, a Gaggia
coffee maker

in the kitchen of women
they left out
in the front yard
like spent equipment

Must we write a poem
about this, o Muse? How
do we even begin?

Once begun, how to —
can you? —
go on, etc.

THE RITES OF MOLOCH

Somebody's kid
slits another kid's throat

Somebody's kid's
throat is slit by another's kid

What, the kids jeer on
Never had your throat slit before?

What, the kids keep on
Never lost your head before?

Gamy kids, somebody's kids
in the wilderness

offered all that a war can give
taking it in

large empty eyes
stacked on the platter like bonbons

What of the kid forced to devour its own raw arm?
What of the kid boiled in its mother's milk?

They look in the ruins of buildings, behind
scorched mutilated trees

dancing around the mine fields —
a secretive hide-and-seek

victim in search of victim
passing through fire

RECIPROCITY

Here, hold this line
tugging gently on
secretive heart, submerged
under a sheet of ice

If I witness your death
will you witness mine
just one time
my beloved

THE MUSE OF HISTORY

History, too, is an art
with a history, date of birth, a geolocation
indexing its emergence

Clio — the daughter of Memory
the eternal falling of the lot
blood-stained weaving of fate with story

Yet more ancient still is Urania —
so the poet, looking up and up
to the stars!

Maybe I'm growing cold
to this writhing inside the war
within the wound?

What if the smell of flesh
decomposing
doesn't reach all the way

to the top of this mount
from which we mouth
verses we've memorised

from the volumes composed
by the men who died
in their own beds

singing the wrath of the demi-gods
of the raging plagues
of convenient, well-administered

cleansings & massacres
heads madly rolling
down the slope of syntax

into the cleft of a poem
mutely vocative
ravenously accusative

INNER FEAST

Tired of being tired of
the unstoppable force

Uncoiling in my lap
a pretty snake

Biting like irony
festering like remorse

Thirsting after my core
entering my navel

BEYOND DEFIANCE

When a voice finds its might
rising out of the well
where it had been hurled
by a nameless force

When a slow-opening flower
breaks up the night
with its curving, tenacious petals
and begs for water

When a mother and a daughter
huddle behind a door
holding cold, clammy hands
as the strangers enter

When we suckle on hope —
a straw in the bitter sea
that no words can contain
no mouths dare utter

LESSONS IN STOICISM

Not as a shadow
but as an altered being
I linger in the world —
a sacred animal
moved off its axis
by an exacting fate

I grew wings
and learned to levitate
ever so slightly
over the creaky boards of
the cellar where I hide
from missiles & bombs

Of my own volition
I choose not to die
but I could have chosen
to die or yet
another option
out of a rich range

of alternatives

ECHOES FROM THE ODYSSEY

When the air raid's over
I still hear them: sirens

airing their wings
on the ghostly boulders of buildings
swelling out of the morning mist

War is warm this year, yet
they're wearing icy armour
each feather frozen —

a cut-throat razor or
a delicate rounded coin
with a protruding spine

Merciless, guiltlessly
unabating, sirens
sing when I close my eyes

stinging them from the inside
with icy quills

DUCK-RABBIT

a field, dry reeds
a patch of ice

like a blot of ink —
a child on the ground

bright red on white
her arms reaching out

shot dead or
making a snow angel?

GENESIS

Dark are the days ahead of us
and even darker — the nights

Hear it said: there'll never
be light again

Sun will blacken and fall
like a corpse of a god

distant, long dead
tossed by the tide of the sky

No more radiance — only
blank and inverted light

Ever darker — the night
every night, darker and darker

Drawn to a close, narrowing
into a point, warmth

seeps out of the world, and we sense
deep inside us — a flutter

an opening up, like a wet
fragile butterfly breaking out of

its tomb of
a second skin —

a word — a formula
once it's all over — for

how to begin
again

KINGDOM OF ENDS

In the brief intermission between
world wars
we somehow managed

to weave a language
out of the things we felt
mattered
for our future
as an impermanent species

Barely even words but
collections of signals from
distant planes of existence, patterns

expressive of a communion between
roots and surfaces, sprawling networks of
fungi, projectiles of spores

shooting out like smart
self-navigating missiles

propagating a form of rebirth
that would touch us all

impartially, indiscriminately

APPROXIMATIONS

Waking up in a borrowed room, in a body
borrowed for a time, in a time
borrowed and hardly used

I remember how light
my head becomes when the boys overtaking us
in the alley tickle me with guns

running them down my spine, then my hip
How I levitate, the force of a scream suppressed
lifting me up and up!

And the way it gets dark when strange men
pound on my door at night
shouting 'Open up, or we'll break it in!'

Right before the war, I'd wake up in bed
dreaming of another bed, body in it exposed
bone by bone, like a radiograph

through a brilliance, an explosion
tearing at the membranes
that ensconce the sleeper

Close, yet not
an exact match, like a rhyme in a poem
you compose posthaste, lines

blurred by terror

AMBUSH

In the hollow of a street
we pause, like travellers entering
a deserted city

Nobody here, but in windows —
shadows, an occasional
ghostly face

afterimages
of a life
there once was

Famished pigeons
surround us
a wall of wings

closing in on
two featherless bipeds
bearing gifts:

seeds, the brittle
bread we grew
in an untidy kitchen

Rubble takes off from
the sidewalk, scraps of tarp
billow jubilantly

Forming a chorus, we dance
crumbs flying up
like confetti

ACKNOWLEDGEMENTS

Grateful acknowledgements are due to the editors of the publications where some of these poems first appeared: *AGNI*, *The Arkansas International*, *Chicago Quarterly Review*, *The Cincinnati Review*, *The Common*, *Conduit*, *The Continental Literary Magazine*, *Copper Nickel*, *Grain Magazine*, *The Indianapolis Review*, *The Manhattan Review*, *Ninth Letter*, *The Paris Review*, *Pleiades*, *Plume*, *PN Review*, *Poetry Ireland Review*, *Poetry London*, *Poetry Northwest*, *The Poetry Review*, *PRISM International*, *Salamander*, *Smartish Pace*, *Southern Indiana Review*, and *The Irish Times*.

I would like to thank Sasha Dugdale, Rachel DeWoskin, Rachel Galvin, and Michael Schmidt for reading the manuscript.

Grateful thanks to the Institute for Advanced Study at the Central European University in Budapest, to the Institute for Human Sciences in Vienna, and to the programmes of Creative Writing and Translation Studies at the University of Chicago for the residencies and fellowships that enabled me to work on this book.

The final stanza of "Rose" contains a quote from G.W.F. Hegel's Preface to the *Philosophy of Right* (1820): 'Here is the rose, here dance', a playful mistranslation of the Latin aphoristic expression *Hic Rhodus, hic salta.*

"Marquise of O" is the title of a novella by Heinrich von Kleist, published in 1808.

The opening lines of "Puppets of God" paraphrase a locution from "The Love Song of J. Alfred Prufrock" (1915) by T.S. Eliot.